Soundless Cries Don't Lead To Healing:

A Critical Thinking Guide to Cultural Consciousness

SOUNDLESS CRIES DON'T LEAD TO HEALING

Printed in the United States of America
ISBN 978-0-692-73342-4
Ingram Spark, 2016
Manhattan, New York
10033

www.ValenciasGarden.com

Dedicated to
my grandmother – Delorise Clay,
my aunt – Hattie L. Purefoy,
and my brother and sister –
Algernon and Kandacy.
Thank you for teaching me the meaning of unconditional love through your understanding,
patience, and honest (sometimes hard) conversations.

To my beloved students,
past, present, and future – thank you for your Light.
I love you.

To the educators who cannot ignore what is going on in the world –
teach on and on and on!

Your Silence
will NOT
PROTECT
You.

-AUDRE LORDE

PREFACE

My intention for creating *Soundless Cries Don't Lead to Healing* was to give the light-makers of the world a plethora of strategies to use with those who look to them for light. These light-makers include but are not limited to educators, doctors, psychologists, caregivers, spiritual leaders, writers, activists, musicians, artists, and anyone in between. What I found during the process of creating this guide of critical-thinking resources was that these strategies could be completed by anyone seeking truth and light; having a facilitator was not necessary.

As an educator, it is disheartening and depressing to see so many of my people, young and old, jumping on bandwagons with no idea of the root of our world's problems, no sense of what is true and what is being sensationalized, no direction on how to obtain a higher level of consciousness for themselves. *Soundless Cries Don't Lead to Healing* is the artillery for a full out combat against the hype-cycle that always seems to subside a week after one of our own is slain. Outside of the few activists that have dedicated their lives to service, we as a society of people who say we want justice, take the usual measures of protesting or posting pictures on social media and <u>then, we go back to living in our bubbles of oblivion</u>, until we are informed by mass media about something egregious occurring again. We are living in times of confusion, a prevalent confusion that yields misperceptions, misjudgments, and misplaced frustration. Rather than unraveling, the malignant rope that tightens the grip on this societal affliction continues to choke us silent. Not to shade the efforts of any leader choosing to speak on our behalf, despite our disconcerted state of taciturnity, but some of the most influential voices seem to have the most minuscule perspectives. This, I consider, silent to the solution. Though a great many people may rally around the cause, they don't realize that their efforts are doing more to ensure that it remains the cause, not the resolution.

We see. We internalize. We scream. We cry. While internalizing, we begin to personalize and persecute ourselves into guilt or shame because of what we see. Screaming, protesting, and uprising to be heard tends to be the abatement of our woes, yet, we find such comfort to be temporary. It dwindles because we do not feel heard. We must consider why we seem to be ignored... Are we unorganized? Are we acting on an emotional level and not a conscious level? Are we equipped with enough knowledge to fuel our power? Until these questions can be asked and answered by us all, there shall be no relief. So we weep – in silence, in fear, and in defense of our feelings.

Instead of merely accepting what we see, we must search, find, and pull the roots of each seed of ignorance that has been planted. If we want a healing for our world, we have to denounce our silence, guilt, and shame. We must stand in solidarity.

Soundless Cries Don't Lead to Healing is broken into two parts. Each part consists of divergent questions, graphic organizers, and space for reflection. Part One starts with self. Before coming together with anyone, we have to do the work of finding ourselves by facing our invisible masks, assessing our personal contributions to community, asking the tough questions that lead to a greater sense of cultural consciousness, and developing a critical eye that will always allow us to think for self. Once we have contended with who we are as individuals, we will be able to question and converse with others. Dialogue will not always be easy but it is a crucial aspect of the healing and growing process.

Comfort zones come secondary to learning. Part Two of this guide provides tools for respectful disagreements and ways to identify opportunities to push us beyond learned biases. Without communication, there is no understanding. Unlike the self-reflection, inquiry, and critical thinking tasks of part one, the dialogue prompts in part two require a partner or a group; they cannot be completed alone. They may be used in a classroom, house-gathering, coffee shop, or in the car on a road trip. Take them everywhere.

While exploring, exchanging, and considering new perspectives through dialogue, we must remember to be true to self. Information should continue to be questioned. Once there is a sense of achievement in kindling a productive discourse that balances our individual ideologies while upholding diversity, we will have the power to heal others in the same way that we have healed ourselves — through mirrors of enlightenment and windows that project empathy and love.

Soundless Cries Don't Lead to Healing is meant to be an independent-exploration guide for those on the journey toward a cultural awareness that will bring out the necessary responsiveness and understanding that is required to possess and share before we can begin to advocate for a true change.

As light-makers, our goal is to perpetuate parity and close the gap that has kept people apart. We know that the only way to wage a successful warfare against ignorance is to educate. I have included a reference list of suggested books, specific excerpts, and scholarly articles to supplement each prompt. Many of these reads have had a substantial influence on the expansion of my consciousness. I am encouraging this literature and the self-discovery of materials beyond this list. As a life-long learner, I have found that my greatest aha-moments of awakening occurred when I was given the freedom to find out for myself. Challenge yourself and those that you may use these strategies with to research unfamiliar words, concepts, and tough questions. Trust me, the information is out there waiting for you to learn and in turn, share with as many open ears as you can.

Before diving into each strategy, it is my recommendation that the pre-work, which was designed to be a mirror of writing reflections, be completed with open and honest responses. If completing these activities with young people, assure them that their reflections will not be judged at all, whatsoever. It is important to set norms that give everyone the assurance that this is a safe space for learning. At the end of the two sections, I recommend completing the summative reflection, which if compared to the pre-work, provide a measurement of growth toward the greater understanding of self and others.

Above all, recognize and recharge the power of your light.
Soundless cries do not lead to healing, use your voice.

AFFIRMATIONS

I am who I am.

✷ I am a light maker. ✷

I am awakened.

I am in alignment with my purpose.

I am a creative being with an ever-emerging momentum of big ideas.

I stand in solidarity with all who desire change.

✷ I use my voice to uplift others in an informed and nonjudgmental manner. ✷

I work from a solutions-oriented stance.

I possess the power to heal.

I am reticent and my silence is thoughtful, never fearful.

I seek and praise diversity.

I am expanding in my emergence of truth.

I act on a conscious level, not an emotional level.

I am revolutionary, not reactionary.

I am free, working to help others find their own freedom.

✷ I am always seeking and asking. I am always finding and learning. ✷

5

WHAT ARE MY PERSONAL BELIEFS?

✓ GENDER ROLES

RACISM

SELF

CHANGE

COMMUNITY

WHAT IT MEANS TO BE A PERSON OF COLOR

POWER

WHAT IT MEANS TO BE CONSIDERED WHITE

WHAT HAS SHAPED MY BELIEFS?

Think back to earliest memories with the concepts of racism, change, power, what it means to be a person of color, what it means to be white, gender-roles, and community. Write a reflection on how your experiences have shaped your beliefs about one or more of the concepts that resonates with you most.

_____

_____

_____

_____

_____

_____

_____

_____

_____

WE ARE NOT ALONE

I am angry about _____
_____.

I am defensive about _____
_____
_____.

I am disgusted with _____
_____
_____.

I am annoyed by _____
_____
_____.

I am confused as to why _____
_____
_____.

I don't know what to say
about _____
_____
_____.

I blame _____
_____
_____.

I _____
_____.

AM I WRONG FOR MY FEELINGS?

SELF-REFLECTION QUESTIONS:

What are my true feelings about the issues of today?
Have I taken the time to contend with my truths?
Am I wrong for my feelings?

"In a time of universal deceit —
telling the truth is a
revolutionary act."
— George Orwell

Being honest with myself about my
true feelings is not wrong, it is
_____
_____.

Now that I have acknowledged
my truths, I am ready to _____
_____
_____.

OWN TRAUMA, RELEASE PAIN

SELF-REFLECTION QUESTIONS:

What is race-based traumatic stress?
How does owning and redefining our trauma help us to release our pain?

TRAUMATIC EXPERIENCES I HAVE ENDURED OR WITNESSED

THE POSITIVE ASPECTS

"ANYTHING THAT WORKS AGAINST YOU CAN ALSO WORK FOR YOU ONCE YOU UNDERSTAND THE PRINCIPLE OF REVERSE." MAYA ANGELOU

I used to consider my traumatic experiences _____
_____

Now I have _____
_____ . 11

Face Fear, Find Strength

Fear doesn't shut you DOWN, it wakes you UP.

-Veronica Roth

SELF-REFLECTION QUESTIONS:

How does avoiding fear widen the gap between ignorance and understanding?

How does living in fear diminish our power?

How can overcoming fear result in gaining strength?

I am afraid to say or do...

The root of my fear is...

In facing my fear I may gain...

I no longer fear _____

because _____.

Why do we hide behind masks?
What steps do we have to take in order to remove our masks?
What is the relationship between removing masks and rebuilding trust?

Break Masks, Build Trust

My mask hides...

My mask leads people to believe...

"We all wear masks and the time comes when we cannot remove them without removing some of our own skin."
— Andre Berthiaume

When I take off my mask, I see...

I want others to see...

Autonomy and Community

SELF-REFLECTION QUESTIONS:

How can I achieve autonomy?

As a community, are we truly liberated?

How can we use our individual freedom to continue to free our community?

I need to free myself from

Once I am free, I can

"The function of freedom is to free someone else." -Toni Morrison

I have let go of bondage and picked up _____

_____

_____.

This impacts my community because _____

_____

_____.

WHITE GUILT, BLACK SHAME

SELF-REFLECTION QUESTIONS:

What is 'white guilt'?
What is 'black shame'?

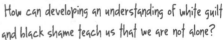

How can developing an understanding of white guilt
and black shame teach us that we are not alone?

WHITE GUILT

BLACK SHAME

" Shame corrodes the very part of us that believes we are
capable of change."   - Brene Brown

After acknowledging my own shame or guilt, I am led to _____
_____.

15

YOU WON'T KNOW
WHAT YOU DON'T KNOW
UNTIL YOU ASK

Question Everything, Always

INQUIRY QUESTIONS:

How do I develop an analytical eye when reading or viewing information?
What kinds of questions will lead me to a higher level of consciousness?

THIN
Answers can be found in the text.

THICK
Answers can be found with research outside of the text.

DEEP
Cannot be answered without raising another question.

Who...

What...

Where...

When...

How did...

Why...

Why not...

What would happen if...

How can we...

What is the solution...

As you read, ask as many questions of the text as you can think of. Sort your questions in the thick, thin, deep categories as you go.

WHAT SHOULD I LOOK FOR?

INQUIRY QUESTIONS:

What patterns or trends can be identified after closely analyzing a source,

i/e: articles social media posts, informational texts, etc.?

Are there hidden biases behind the presentation of the source?

What is the motive, intent, or purpose of the source that I am viewing?

Is the source using language that generalizes a specific group of people?

Is the source recounting events objectively or subjectively?

Who is the intended audience?

What implications will this text or post have on the way their audience views the subject of the text or post?

"The media, itself an arm of mega-corporate power, feeds the fear industry, so that people are primed like pumps to support wars on rumor, innuendo, legends, and lies." - Mumia Abu-Jamal

Being analytical and remaining inquisitive when viewing media will allow me to _____.

19

INQUIRY QUESTIONS:

How do I define cultural-competence?
Are some people born with culturally-competence?
What is the correlation between making generalized statements and being ignorant?
What have I said or not said as a result of my own misperception of others?

IGNORANCE & CULTURAL AWARENESS

General Assumptions or Stereotypes I think about others	The Truth	Reliable Source

"... racial competence must be learned and everyone that has it learned it the hard way." - Ali Michael

Having a growth mindset about my ability to become culturally competent has allowed me to _____.

WHITE RESPONSIBILITY, BLACK POWER

INQUIRY QUESTIONS:

What is white responsibility?
What is black power?
How can white privilege enable white responsibility?
How does black affirmation create black power?
How does acknowledging our power and privilege strengthen or separate us?

ON THE LEFT, LIST WAYS THE WORDS IN EACH ARROW BENEFITS YOU.
ON THE RIGHT, LIST WAYS THE WORDS IN EACH ARROW BENEFITS OTHERS

"Privilege exists when one group has something of value that is denied of others simply because of the groups they belong to, rather than because of anything they failed to do. Power from unearned privilege can look like strength when it is in fact permission to escape or to dominate."
-Peggy McIntosh

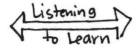
Access & Privelige

Listening to Learn

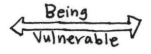
Being Vulnerable

I will hold myself accountable for the most responsible use of my

_____

_____

_____

_____

_____

_____

_____

_____

21

SHOULD I CHOOSE A SIDE?

I feel strongly about...	Why?	Sources for Others to Learn More About My Perspective

"We must always take sides. Neutrality helps the oppressor, never the victim. Silence encourages the tormentor, never the tormented." -Elie Wiesel

I choose to stand for _____.

READING (AND LISTENING) WITH A CRITICAL EYE

CRITICAL-THINKING QUESTIONS:

How does mainstream-media influence a person's perception of others?
Why does society accept the narratives that mainstream-media provides?
How do I evaluate a source while reading?
How do I evaluate a person's argument?

> "Read not to contradict or confute; nor to believe and take for granted; nor to find talk and discourse, but to weigh and consider."
> -Francis Bacon

Implicit Implications ⟶ Evidence	
Motive, Intent, or Author's Purpose	
Generalized Statements	
Subjective Language	
Bias Statements	

Consciously developing my critical eye will allow me to _____

25

CRITICAL-THINKING QUESTIONS:

How do I continue to grow my knowledge?
Why is it important to continuing searching for answers,
even after I have found one?

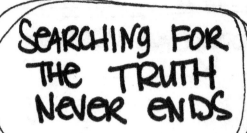

SEARCHING FOR THE TRUTH NEVER ENDS

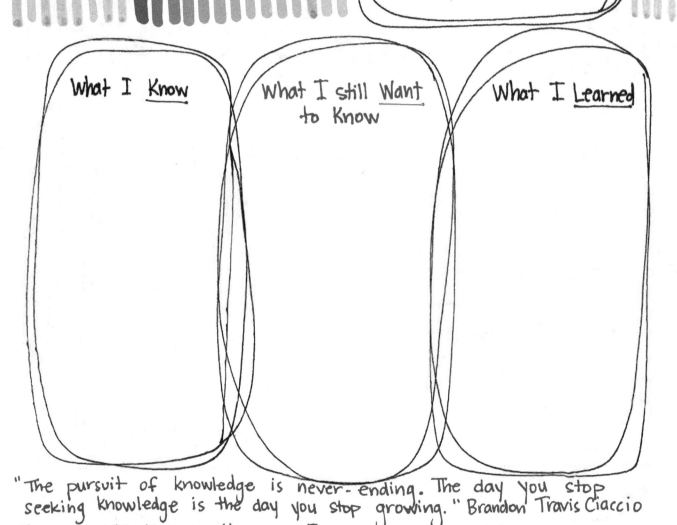

What I Know

What I still Want to Know

What I Learned

"The pursuit of knowledge is never-ending. The day you stop seeking knowledge is the day you stop growing." Brandon Travis Ciaccio

The more I discover, the more I _____

What are ideas that I have subscribed to without realizing that they don't align with what I know?

How have my personal experiences impacted what I know?

How can I stay true to myself?

Topic	"They" Say...	But I Know
Black Lives Matter		
All Lives Matter		
All Police are Prejudice		

If I jump on a bandwagon instead of thinking for myself, I will _____

_____

_____

THEY SAY... BUT I KNOW...

You possess the
Power to
Heal

DIALOGUE! DIALOGUE! DIALOGUE!

DIALOGUE QUESTIONS:

How does dialogue benefit our community as a whole?

What is the outcome of failing to communicate?

How do we engage in a productive discourse, even if we disagree?

Why should we use literature to back our claims?

"The purpose of an argument should not be victory but progress."

-Anonymous

Use the following "Accountable Talk" sentence starters when engaging in the discussion-protocols:

Being Respectful

I agree... because...

I would like to respectfully disagree...

I understand your point of view but from my perspective...

Remaining Relevant

According to...

From what I have read...

To connect back to what you said, an example is...

Sounding Intelligent

Use of proper grammar

Appropriately inserting power words

Asking questions to gain understanding and deepen the dialogue

Use ideas from others to add to your own

The greatest benefit of engaging in dialogue is

CARE TO SHARE

DIALOGUE PROTOCOL

Purpose:

To allow participants to share their thoughts and listen to others.

May be used in addition to other protocols.

Provides a sense of mutual respect.

Steps:

After reading, watching a video, etc., break into a small group or in pairs.

1. Each person shares their thoughts individually.

2. The other group members respond with the sentence starter, "I care about you shared because…"

3. Repeat rounds.

Debriefing Questions:

How did sharing and listening broaden your perspective on the subject?

How did listening to someone describe why they care about you think make you feel?

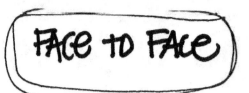

FACE TO FACE

DIALOGUE PROTOCOL

Purpose:

To allow participants to generate thoughts or questions.

Steps:

This activity requires to stand or sit in two parallel rows, face to face with a partner.

1. The person in the left row gives their partner sitting across from them in the right row a compliment.

2. The partner responds with a compliment to the person.

3. Both continue to go back and forth, compliment for compliment.

4. After 30 seconds, the facilitator will signal the group to rotate the row. This rotation will allow partners to switch.

5. Repeat rounds.

Variations: This protocol can be done with questions for questions, word for word, or other specific topics.

Debriefing Questions:

What was the impact that saying things face to face have on you?

What were some of the challenges?

7 INSIGHTFUL QUESTIONS

DIALOGUE PROTOCOL

Purpose:

These questions are a great window to getting to know a person. The answers can reveal aspects of a person's life that helps explain their personal perspective on bigger issues.

Steps:

1. In small groups or with a partner, participants should answer the following questions:

    What is the origin of your name?

    How did your parents meet?

    What is your learning style?

    Who challenges you the most?

    What is your definition of success?

    Where do find yourself to be most at peace?

    Why do you work?

2. Participants can answer questions one at a time, going around or each participant can go through each other questions without stopping.

3. Participants can ask questions after each person answers the questions. Participants should not answer questions until everyone in the group has shared.

Debriefing Questions:

How does knowing about a person's background help us to gain a shared understanding on their perspective of the world today?

ON PAPER v. REALITY

Purpose:

Allows participants to explain concepts from their perspective.

Allows participants to form a common language around broad topics.

Steps:

1. As a group, generate a list of power words like the list below:

Progress   Empowerment   Freedom
Privilege   Equality   Power   Class   Empathy
Resistance   Equity   Awareness   Bias
Oppressor   Agency   Change
Community   Liberation
Leadership   Advocacy   Progress

2. The facilitator can choose one word for the group(s) to discuss or each participant can choose one word that resonates with them most.

3. Each discussion should allow participants to first identify the definition of the word.

4. Each participant shares what the word looks like in reality, despite its definition.

5. Following the last step, participants come up with what they desire the concept of the word to look like and what they can do to support this desire.

Debriefing Questions:

How did this discussion support the idea that we are the creators of our own reality?

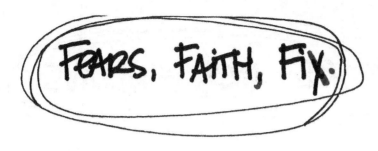

FEARS, FAITH, FIX.

DIALOGUE PROTOCOL

Purpose:

Allows participants to develop solutions for issues they are struggling with confronting.

Steps:

1. Facilitator chooses an issue or topic of focus.

2. Each participant shares their

    -Fears about the topic

    -Hopes or what they faith may change or happen as a positive result of the topic

    -Ways in which they can contribute to fixing the issue

3. The participants develop an outline of an action plan that they may use to follow up on progress toward fixing the issue.

Debriefing Questions:

What are some challenges that may hinder us from moving forward?

How can we be proactive about the challenges?

MIRRORS AND WINDOWS

DIALOGUE PROTOCOL

Purpose:

Allows all participants to understand everyone's individual perspectives

Steps:

Facilitator may choose the topic of focus.

1. In a whole group or small groups, each person shares their mirror or personal view of the topic and how their personal life experiences have shaped those views. This may require individual reflection time before sharing out loud.

2. As each person listens, they are being offered a window to understanding each other's perspective.

3. Participants ask whole group questions, not personal questions, which the group may answer as a discussion to further expand perspective.

Debriefing Questions:

What did we learn about one another?

What did we learn from one another?

What do we need to unlearn?

CONFRONTING GENERALIZATIONS

DIALOGUE PROTOCOL

Purpose:

Participants will be able to share their struggles with generalizations.

Participants will learn what others feel when being type-casted.

Participants will see who they become when they make generalizations.

Steps:

1. Participants should reflect using the sentence starters below

    People assume that I...

    It makes me feel ...

    I want them to understand....

    When I make generalized statements like...

    It makes me sound ...

    I realize...

2. After each person shares their truths other participants can ask questions on note cards or sticky notes

3. Participants can choose which questions they would like to answer out loud, if any.

Debriefing Questions:

How does confronting generalizations help us to heal as a culture?

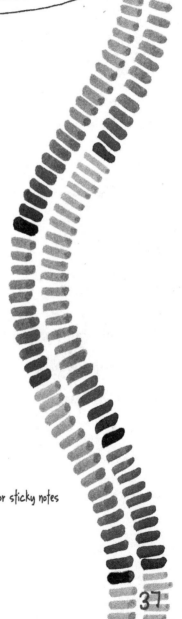

SHADOWS AND LIGHT

Purpose:

To find the positive aspects in every situation

Steps:

1. Participants should reflect using two sentence starters

   What I lost...

   What I learned...

2. Each participant shares their responses.

3. Participants share things they learned from other people's losses and lessons.

Debriefing Questions:

How do we find the good in everything?

How do we turn a loss into a lesson?

How does knowing what we don't want bring us closer to what we do want?

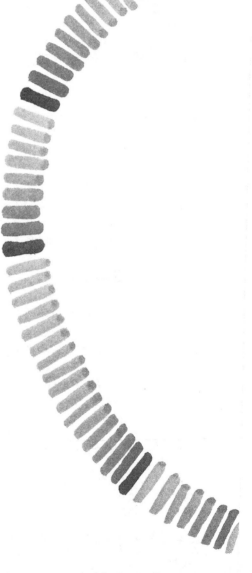

LIST AND LEARN

DIALOGUE PROTOCOL

Purpose:

To learn about the way others view themselves

Steps:

1. Each person generates a list of 10 words that describes themselves

2. Each person goes around and shares their list without explaining

3. After each person has shared their list, participants can go around and share the reasoning behind 3 of the words that the group chooses to know more about.

Debriefing Questions:

How did this activity allow you to understand one another more?

30/30 LiFE STORiES

DIALOGUE PROTOCOL

Purpose:

To learn about where a person comes from and how that impacts their actions today

Steps:

1. With a partner, each person has 30 seconds to share everything they can about their life.

2. Once each pair has shared, the whole group comes back together to form a circle.

3. Each person uses one word to describe their partner's life.

Debriefing Questions:

How did this activity help us to be more mindful of the diversity and similarities that we share with one another?

What did we learn about one another?

What did we learn from one another?

What do we need to unlearn?

DIALOGUE PROTOCOL

Purpose:

To develop awareness of differences and similarities

Steps:

1. Facilitator calls out different categories for participants to move and self-form their own groups:

    Birth month

    College major or favorite subject in school

    Book genre

    Political party

    Gender

    Ethnicity

    Nationality

    Race

2. As each group forms, participants should discuss:

    Why did you identify yourself in this way?

    What does it mean to be _____?

    One thing we would like the other groups to know about us is _____?

Debriefing Questions:

How did it feel to be in each group?

What were the successes and challenges of this activity?

THE FIRST TIME

DIALOGUE PROTOCOL

Purpose:

Allows participants to reflect on their experiences while allowing others to gain insight

Steps:

1. Facilitator may provide a list of words that label experiences such as: racism, failure, chauvinism, heartbreak, success, freedom, independence, success

2. Participants share their own narrative, starting off with, "The first time I experienced _____ was _____. The impact it still has on me today is_____." Participants should be given 1-2 minutes each to share.

3. After everyone has shared, participants should make connections to other people's narratives by saying, "I can relate to _____"

4. Finally, specific questions can be raised and answered.

Debriefing Questions:

What was successful about this discussion?

HOW MANY LIKES DID IT GET?

DIALOGUE PROTOCOL

Purpose:

To analyze images and raise questions that may drive a discussion around important issues

Steps:

This activity can be completed with images, headlines, or thought-provoking quotes. Facilitator must do the pre-work of hanging many photos, headlines, or quotes around the room.

1. Participants can view the images and write what they notice and wonder about each.

2. After viewing all of the images, each participant may leave one sticker on the image to indicate their interest in learning more about it.

3. Once the image that has the most stickers or "likes" is identified, the facilitator can begin a discussion about the things the group noticed and wondered about the image.

Debriefing Questions:

What steps can we take to continue analyzing the issue or questions raised in this discussion?

How did the image shift your perspective on the issue?

43

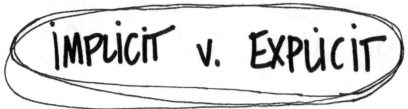

IMPLICIT v. EXPLICIT

DIALOGUE PROTOCOL

Purpose:

To identify implicit messages in literature, movies, images, or music.

Steps:

Choose the content that will be analyzed. For example, the song "Forbidden Knowledge" by Raury and Big Krit. For more examples, see appendix.

1. Play the song.

2. Play the song again, allowing participants to view the lyrics.

3. Prompt participants to close read and annotate the lyrics for inferred meaning and thin/thick/deep questions

4. Each participant shares their inferences about the implicit messages that were discovered. Facilitator should write these on chart paper for the whole group to reference when needed.

5. Each participant shares their questions. Facilitator should write these on chart paper for the whole group to reference when needed.

6. After everyone has shared, participants choose the top 3 questions that they would like explore within an open discussion. Participants should be prompted to use accountable-talk during discussion.

Debriefing Questions:

How do implicit messages give us insight on deep issues?

RECORD, ANALYZE, EVALUATE, GROW

DIALOGUE PROTOCOL

Purpose:

The purpose of recording your conversations is to reflect on what was said and identify areas of growth.

Steps:

1. Record the discussion

2. Assign a group member to take anecdotal notes

3. After the discussion, type the dialogue so that each participant may analyze and evaluate the dialogue for:

   -Evidence of accountable-talk: respectfulness, relevance, and intelligence

   -Places in the conversation where there may be a need for more evidence to support a claim and strengthen the argument

4. Care-to-Share thoughts and findings with the group so that   participants may grow.

Debriefing Questions:

How does evaluating our discussions align with the idea of having a growth mindset?

45

POST REFLECTION
OPERATIONALIZING THE KNOWLEDGE

In what ways has your cultural consciousness been enhanced? How will you use this knowledge to begin healing our community?

_____

_____

_____

_____

_____

_____

_____

_____

_____

_____

47

 # RESOURCES

Articles and Essays:

A Last Word Before Incarceration — Marcus Garvey

A Talk to Teachers — James Baldwin

Colored Men Standing in the Way of their Own Race — James Lynch

Coping While Black: A Season Of Traumatic News Takes A Psychological Toll - Cheryl Corley

Definitions of Black Power — Stokely Carmichael

From White Guilt to White Responsibility - Hannah Adair Bonner

Letter from Birmingham City Jail — Martin Luther King, Jr.

Moving Beyond Shame — bell hooks

My Class Didn't Trump My Race

Poetry is Not a Luxoury — Audre Lorde

Racism's Psychological Toll - Jenna Wortham

The Ballot or the Bullet — Malcolm X

The Case for Reparations - Ta-Nehisi Coates

The Transformation of Silence into Language and Action — Audre Lorde

We Are at War — Sister Souljah

We Wear the Mask — bell hooks

We're On Our Way — Fannie Lou Hamer

What it Means to be Colored in the Capitol of the US — Mary Church Terrell

What to the Slave is the 4th of July? — Frederick Douglass

White Privilege: Unpacking the Invisible Knapsack — Peggy McIntosh

Books:

A Lesson Before Dying - Ernest J. Gaines

A Raisin in the Sun - Lorraine Hansberry

A Taste of Power - Elaine Brown

African Origin of Civilization — Myth or Reality - Cheikh Anta Diop

Always Running — Luis J. Rodríguez

Americanah - Chimamanda Ngozi Adichie

Animal Farm - George Orwell

Assata - Assata Shakur

Articulate While Black: Barack Obama, Language, and Race in the U.S. - H. Samy Alim

Autobiography of Angela Davis — Angela Davis

Between the World and Me - Ta-Nehisi Coates

Bird of Paradise — Raquel Cepeda

Black Boy — Richard Wright

Black Face, White Mask — Frantz Fanon

Black Marxism: The Making of the Black Radical Tradition - Cedric J. Robinson

Black Protest - Joanne Grant

Blue Print for Black Power - Amos N. Wilson

Blood in My Eye - George L. Jackson

Colorblind: The Rise of Post-Racial Politics and the Retreat from Racial Equity — Tim Wise

Critical Race Theory: An Introduction - Richard Delgado and Jean Stefancic

Feminism is for Everybody - bell hooks

Fences - August Wilson

For Colored Girls Who Have Considered Suicide When the Rainbow Is Enuf - Ntozake Shange

Go Tell it on the Mountain - James Baldwin

How Jews Became White Folks and What That Says About Race in America - Karen Brodkin

How the Garcia Girls Lost their Accents - Julia Alvarez

Invisible Man - Ralph Ellison

Lies My Teacher Told Me: Everything Your American History Textbook Got Wrong - James W. Loewen

Makes Me Wanna Holler - Nathan McCall

Manchild in the Promise Land - Claude Brown

Native Son - Richard Wright

Of Poetry and Protest: From Emmett Till to Trayvon Martin - Phil Cushway and Michael Warr

Pedagogy of the Oppressed - Paulo Freire

Post Traumatic Slave Syndrome - Joy Angela Degruy

Racism without Racists: Color-Blind Racism and the Persistence of Racial Inequality in America

Raising Race Questions - Whiteness and Inquiry in Education - Ali Michael

Salvation - bell hooks

Sister Outsider - Audre Lorde

Slavery by Another Name - Douglas A. Blackmon

Soul on Ice - Eldridge Cleaver

Stolen Legacy - George G M James

Sula - Toni Morrison

The Best Short Stories by Black Writers - Langston Hughes and Gloria Naylor

The Bluest Eye - Toni Morrison

The Fire Next Time - James Baldwin

The Isis Papers - Dr. Frances Cress Welsing

The Long Emancipation – Ira Berlin

The Making and Unmaking of Whiteness – Birgit Brander Rasmussen and Irene J. Nexica

The Mis-Education of the Negro – Carter Godwin Woodson

The Myth of the Negro Past – Melville Herskovits

The New Jim Crow – Michelle Alexander

The Panther and the Lash – Langston Hughes

The Skin That We Speak: Thoughts on Language and Culture in the Classroom – Lisa Delpit & Joanne Kilgour Dowdy

The Souls of Black Folks – W.E.B. Du Bois

The Street – Ann Petry

The Willie-Lynch Letter – Willie Lynch

To Be Young, Gifted, and Black – Lorraine Hansberry

Their Eyes Were Watching God – Zora Neale Hurston

Uprooting Racism: How White People Can Work for Racial Justice – Paul Kivel

What If All the Kids Are White? – Louise Olsen Derman-Sparks and Patricia G. Ramsey

White by Law: The Legal Construction of Race – Ian Haney López

White Like Me: Reflections on Race from a Privileged Son – Tim Wise

White Privilege: Essential Readings on the Other Side of Racism – Paula S. Rothenberg

White Women, Race Matters: The Social Construction of Whiteness – Ruth Frankenberg

Music and Music Videos:

All Falls Down — Kanye West

All the Kings — Add-2

Alright — Kendrick Lamar

America the Beautiful - Homeboy Sandman

American Rapstar - Big K.R.I.T.

American Terrorist — Lupe Fiasco

Around My Way — Lupe Fiasco

Be a Nigger Too — Nas

Be Free — J. Cole

Be No Slave - J-Live

Blacker the Berry — Kendrick Lamar

Blood on the Leaves — Kanye West

Book of Life - Common

Dorian - Brother Ali

Changes - 2Pac

Civil War - Immortal Technique

Crack Music — Kanye West and The Game

Don't Shoot — The Game, et. al.

Dreams - Little Brother

Forbidden Knowledge — Raury and Big Krit

Freedom Time — Lauryn Hill

Guns Under Fire — The Roots

Hell Yeah — Dead Prez

Hard as They Come - Cunninlynguists

Holy Key — DJ Khaled and Big Sean and Kendrick
　　Lamar

How Much a Dollar Really Cost — Kendrick Lamar

Industry - Cormega

Just to Get By — Talib Kweli

Murder to Excellence — Jay-Z and Kanye West

Nas Album Done — DJ Khaled and Nas

Never Let Me Down — Kanye West Verse

New Slaves — Kanye West

New York State of Mind, Pt. II - Nas

Off Da Record - Bossman

Paranoia - Chance the Rapper

Love Ain't - Cunninlynguists

I Get Out — Lauryn Hill

January 28th — J. Cole

Lifting Shadows - Oddisee

Martyrs — Mick Jenkins

Master Teacher Medley — Erykah Badu

Nature of the Threat — Ras Kass

Ni**as in Protest — Yasiin Bey

No More Control - Murs

Penthouse Cloud — The Internet

Reagan — Killer Mike

Redemption Freestyle - Voli

Ruled the World - Natti

SDE - Cam'ron

Say Something - Sha Stimuli

Senorita - Vince Staples

Sly Fox — Nas

Strange Fruition — Lupe Fiasco

Styles P - I'm Black

Sunshine - Pusha T

Talib Kweli - The Proud
That's Life and That's Life 2 - Killer Mike
The Gates - Cunninlynguists
The Light - Common
The Man - Rapsody

The N Word Song – Sha Stimuli
The Saga Remix - Cormega
The Wander Years - Voli
These Words - Raz Simone

They Schools – Dead Prez
This is What's Cool - Mistah F.A.B.

This Bitter Land – Nas and Erykah Badu

To Pimp a Butterfly – Kendrick Lamar

Too High to Riot - BAS

Uncle Sam Goddamn – Brother Ali

Untitled 01 – Kendrick Lamar

UNITY – Queen Latifah
Valley of Death - Cunninlynguists
War - King Los

Weak People – CyHi The Prynce

White Ni**er – Ill Bill

Who We Be – DMX
Wings - Macklemore

Word to the Mother(land) – Big Daddy Kane
Words I Never Said - Lupe Fiasco

Movies and Documentaries:

Africans in America before Columbus

African History vs. Biblical Myth — Ashra Kwesi

American Promise

Boyz N the Hood

Eve's Bayou

Colored Frames

Dare Not Walk Alone

Dark Girls

Dear White People

Do the Right Thing

Emit Till: The Untold Story

Ethnic Notions

Eyes on the Prize

Freedom Riders

Goodbye Uncle Tom

How to De-Activate the Willie Lynch Chip

Malcolm X — Spike Lee

Mama Africa

Marcus Garvey

Mirrors of Privilege: Making Whiteness Visible

Neshoba

Post-Traumatic Slave Syndrome

Race: The Power of an Illusion

The African Americans: Many Rivers to Cross

The African Origin of Civilization and Spiritual Concepts

The Birth of a Nation

The Black List: Volume One

The Black Panthers: Vanguard of the Revolution

The Black Power Mixtape 1967-1975

The Black Wall Street

The Central Park Five

The Color Purple

The Loving Story

The Naked Truth

The Spook Who Sat by the Door

Sankofa

Slavery by Another Name

Soundtrack for a Revolution

Zeitgeist

Visual Artists:

Aaron Maybin

AfriCOBRA

Amirtharaj Stephen

An-My Lê

Archibald Motley

Augusta Savage

Brandan "B-Mike" Odums

Catherine Opie

Debra Cartwright

Devin Allen

Diego Rivera

Faith Ringgold

Glenn Ligon

Gordon Parks

Jacob Lawrence

Jamel Shabazz

Jean-Michel Basquiat

José Climente Orozco

Kadir Nelson

Kara Walker

Kehinde Wiley

Kerry James Marshall

Mary Reid Kelley

Nancy Spero

Nichole Kobi

Nikki Lee

Njideka Akunyili Crosby

Pablo Picasso

Sergi Cámara

Sharla Hammond

Titus Kaphar

Willie Birch

REFERENCES

Berger, L., Mehta, J., Vilen, A., & Woodfin, L. (2016) Learning that lasts: Challenging, engaging, and empowering students with deeper instruction. San Francisco, CA: John Wiley and Sons.

Berger, R., Rugen, L., & Woodfin, L. (2014) Leaders of their own learning: Transforming schools through student-engaged assessment. San Francisco, CA: John Wiley and Sons.

Berger, R. & Woodfin, L. (2014) Transformational literacy: Making the common core shift with work that matters. San Francisco, CA: John Wiley and Sons.

Bonner, H. A. (2015). From white guilt to white responsibility. Retrieved from http://www.ministrymatters.com/all/entry/6153/from-white-guilt-to-white-responsibility. Accessed August 03, 2016.

Dichter, A., McDonald, E. C., Mohr, N., & McDonald, J. P. (2007). The power of protocols: An educator's guide to better practice. New York: Teachers College Press.

McConnell, C. (2011). The essential questions handbook. New York: Scholastic.

Michael, A. (2015). Raising race questions: Whiteness and inquiry in education. New York: Teachers College Press.

Erwin, J. C. (2004). The classroom of choice: Giving students what they need and getting what you want. Alexandria, VA: Association for Supervision and Curriculum Development.

Harvey, S., & Goudvis, A. (2000). Strategies that work: Teaching comprehension to enhance understanding. York, ME: Stenhouse.

Hooks, B. (2003). Rock my soul: Black people and self-esteem. New York: Atria Books.

Mcintosh, P. (2015). Extending the knapsack: Using the white privilege analysis to examine conferred advantage and disadvantage. Women & Therapy, 38(3-4), 232-245.

McIntosh, P. (1998). White privilege: Unpacking the invisible knapsack. Race, class, and gender in the United States: An integrated study.

Williams, M. T. (2013). Can Racism Cause PTSD? Implications for DSM-5. Retrieved from https://www.psychologytoday.com/blog/culturally-speaking/201305/can-racism-cause-ptsd-implications-dsm-5. Accessed August 03, 2016.

Zwiers, J., & Crawford, M. (2011). Academic conversations: Classroom talk that fosters critical thinking and content understandings. Portland, ME: Stenhouse.

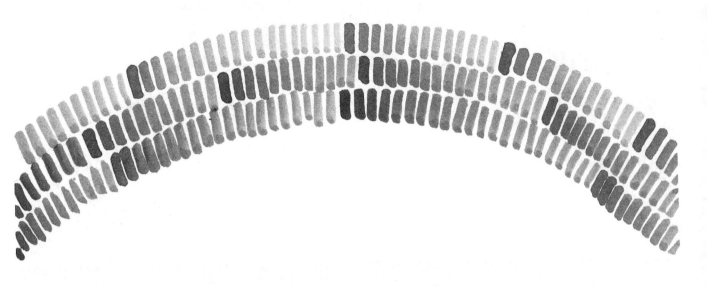

QUESTIONS · WONDERINGS · AHA MOMENTS · THOUGHTS · EPIPHANIES

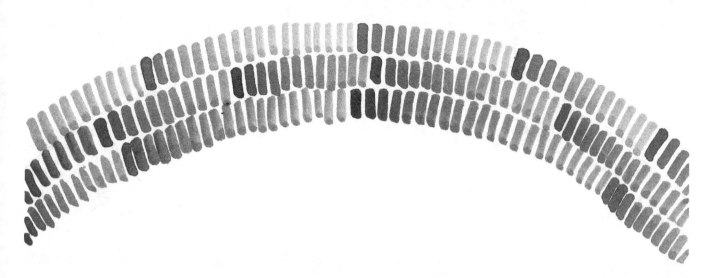

QUESTIONS · WONDERINGS · AHA MOMENTS · THOUGHTS · EPIPHANIES

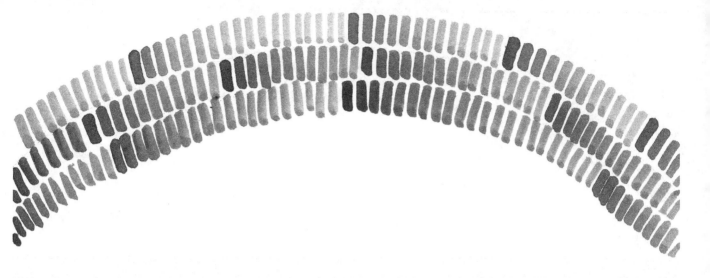

QUESTIONS · WONDERINGS · AHA MOMENTS · THOUGHTS · EPIPHANIES

QUESTIONS · WONDERINGS · AHA MOMENTS · THOUGHTS · EPIPHANIES

CPSIA information can be obtained
at www.ICGtesting.com
Printed in the USA
LVHW060126070519
616790LV00009B/922/P